Life Poems

Lydia Marshall

Presentation by *BookLeaf Publishing*

Web: www.bookleafpub.com

E-mail: info@bookleafpub.com

ISBN: 9789395756365

First edition 2022

Humans and Nature

I step through the gates, locals spring to life.
The leaves sway to the rhythm of the breeze.
Birds sing harmoniously, the mood is right.
Bench warmers bask in the shade of the trees.
Warm smiles, hearty laughter, rekindled flames.
Whooshing wheels break momentary silence.
Boys in the distance playing ball games.
A child bawls, mother deals with defiance.
Joyful Joggers pass by, deeper conversations.
Lonely fields and hills, fountain flows.
I'm amazed by creation.

Reunion

A familiar face
A sundae and carrot cake
Good vibes, feels like home

Heartstrings

Curtains drawn, I'm surrounded by these four walls.
Outside my window, I hear the excited voices of friends reconnecting.
I'm just surrounded by these four walls.
Head bowed, heart sinks, but then I turn to you.
I immerse myself in you.
With you I'm elated, exhilarated, no more frustrated.
You are like the blessing of a cold beverage in sweltering heat.
Like a sudden sunburst, you push the clouds away.
You drown out the noise day by day.
You lay across my lap, I place my hand on your neck and I pluck at your heartstrings.
We get lost in melodies, I lose track of time.

Post-Uni blues

I try my best but it seems my best is not enough.
Is my resume not strong enough?
Am I the weakest in the competition?
Why would I be the weakest in the competition?
I have a wealth of knowledge and experience.
Still they reject me over and over again.
I keep going.
I love my independence, I dread the day that I let
it go.
I keep going.
I step out of my comfort zone, I grab hold of
opportunities.
I attempt to build connections.
Brushing off the discouragement, I renew my
mind.
I keep an open mind, this is not a hopeless
situation.
My faith will rise regardless of the situation.
On Christ the solid rock I stand.
All other ground is sinking sand.

I'm over it

I'm over it.
As I grow older, I grow tired of foolishness.
I grow impatient, praying for patience.
I'm tired of overexerting myself when I'm
undervalued.
I'm tired of repeating myself to people who lack
common decency and good values.
Living with strangers has been draining.
Shout out to my parents for good home training.
I'm tired of doing jobs that I don't enjoy.
I endure condescending people.
They stress over things that are not that deep.
I'm over it.
I know things will turn around but right now, I'm
over it.

Strength

Peace in solitude
Relaxation in leisure
Recuperating

Social media

Social media, there are so many highs and lows.
Validation comes when followers grow.
Constant FOMO.
Everyone appears to be living their best life.
There is a longing to be in their shoes.
We don't see them behind closed doors, if only
we knew.
It's become a routine, scrolling for hours on end.
Neglecting family and friends.
Insecure and anxious.
Isolated and alone.
Bowing to peer pressure, still we're glued to the
phone.
Yearning for human interaction but forgetting
how to interact.
Emotionally detached.
Virtually connected yet physically disconnected.
Capturing moments but not living in them.
Social media also brings joy and laughter.
Opportunities to build and thrive.
Exposure to news and education, many
memories in the archives.
For some it's sentimental
Let's take breaks and protect our mental.

Better days

Better days are coming, so I hold on.
Better days are coming, it won't be long.
Better days are coming, I don't stay down.
Better days are coming, I adjust my crown.
Better days are coming, I lift my head high.
Better days are coming, the limit is the sky.
Better days are coming, I wipe my tears away.
Better days are coming, I will be okay.

Growth

Growth is a process, it takes time
Patience is key
Seasons change, storms don't last forever
Rejection is redirection
Learn and unlearn
Take action, make a move
Failures are teachable moments
They will shape you for success
Don't let fear cripple you
You have so much more to give
You add value, you are valued
A seed becomes a plant
Caterpillars become butterflies
You will become the best version of yourself

Anxiety

I'm the center of attention and I don't want to be.
Sharp as a knife, their eyes pierce me.
Muscles tighten, palms become wet.
I feel trapped like a fish that's caught in a net.
I'm stuck to my seat, the walls are closing in.
Chills dart through the pores of my skin.
Heart palpitations, blurry vision.
Wanting desperately to escape this painful
prison.
Fighting back tears, I don't want to seem weak.
Shaking back fears, but this time I'm beat.
I slip out when no one's looking.
I'm full of regret and frustration.
Puddles of tears from this disturbing invasion.

Summer

Sun rays beat down on my skin.
Watch how it glistens, this sweet melanin.
A breath of fresh air from the grey and gloom.
I catch a vibe to the sounds of my favourite
tunes.
Body breathes when I dispose of winter attire.
Constant showers as the temperature gets higher.
I scream, eyes close as I indulge in the
butterscotch and honeycomb.
It melts in my mouth, it sets the tone.
Trying not to complain when humidity hits.
Moan in every season, life of a Brit.
True summer baby, I embrace it when it
comes.
Gripping tightly because I know it won't last
very long.

90's R&B

12

Singing in the rain
Depth, soulful and melodic
The Rhythm and blues

Affirmations

Rosy reminders
Uplifted and encouraged
Repositioned crown

Training wheels

A small football pitch becomes the training
ground.
That fearful little girl is nowhere to be found.
Dusting herself off she tries again. Internal
flames, hot like cayenne.
This is her moment, determined to shine. She
mounts her ride, she wastes no time. Twists and
turns but she's in control now. She circles the
pitch and wipes the sweat off her brow.
She steers with conviction and now she knows.
There is a release and freedom in finally letting
go.

Time

I would love to turn back time
Reverse and press play
See the loved ones who have left me
Remain in the shelter of their arms
They live on in my memories
They won't be in my future
They are in my past and not my present
I should have loved harder
Loved stronger
Loved deeper
Loved longer
Time waits for no one
I can't waste it!
I must grab it tight before it slips away
I would love to turn back time

Words

Children are like sponges, they soak up what they hear.
Be careful with your words, watch how you speak.
Speak words that edify, show that you care.
Words are engraved recollections.
Children become adults and still they don't forget.
They struggle to build with familiar connections.
Those who should be safe havens are danger zones.
Sometimes protect the heart and love from a distance.
Be the change now that you're grown.
Don't be a reflection of the behaviour you despise.
Live, learn and unlearn.
Think before you speak, be wise.

Rain

17

A surge of cloudburst
Accelerated rainfall
A damp aroma

Faith

In the deepest valley, I lift my eyes towards the highest mountain.
The avalanche cannot bury me, I stand.
Trouble don't last always, I will win.
My shield quenches the fiery darts of the enemy.
My full armour gives me confidence.
I am protected, the test is a testimony.
I will not be overcome by these trials.
I'm an overcomer, more than a conqueror.
Even in sorrow there is revival.
Endurance brings victory.
There is hope, I jump over hurdles.
Joy replaces misery.
Sermons and teachings cause strength to rise.
Uplifting music and scriptures reassure me.
I press towards the mark for the prize.

Graduation

Elated faces
Nervous jitters
Caps and gowns
Anticipation
Appreciation
Smiles all around
Observation
Conversation
Clapping hands
Names mentioned
Cameras snap
Shaking hands
Sigh of relief
Proud parents
Gratitude
Reunited
Reminisce
Positive attitude

Packing

Uprooting again, the confined space overwhelms
me.
Possessions secured in luggage, bags and boxes.
Getting tired, taking breaks, I can't wait to be
free.
Letting go of items to lighten the load.
Baggage is a burden.
Deep breaths so I don't explode.
Tackling this new endeavour.
Self-assured is my mode.
This change I will treasure.

Family

I return home to loving embraces.
Wonderful developments and sentimental
photos.
Habitual banter, cheery faces.
My brothers help me out and make sure I'm
okay.
What a blessing it is to have them.
My parents check up on me when I'm away.
Foolery and theatrics, recycled jokes.
Homecooked meals and catching up.
Acting hard like I want all the smoke.
It feels good to be seen, it feels good to be
appreciated.
I'll give them flowers in life and make sure that
they are celebrated.